T0198397

HIGH-FIVE THROUGH ANXIETY

Dana M. Shickora

Archway Publishing books may be ordered through booksellers or by contacting:

Archway Publishing
1663 Liberty Drive
Bloomington, IN 47403
www.archwaypublishing.com
844-669-3957

Because of the dynamic nature of the Internet, any web addresses or links contained in this book may have changed since publication and may no longer be valid. The views expressed in this work are solely those of the author and do not necessarily reflect the views of the publisher, and the publisher hereby disclaims any responsibility for them.

Any people depicted in stock imagery provided by Getty Images are models, and such images are being used for illustrative purposes only.
Certain stock imagery © Getty Images.

Illustrated by Maryna Salagub

ISBN: 978-1-6657-0777-0 (sc)
ISBN: 978-1-6657-0778-7 (e)

Print information available on the last page.

Archway Publishing rev. date: 06/18/2021

HIGH-FIVE THROUGH ANXIETY

"Sloane, wake up!" Momma called. "It's the first day of school. You're going to be late!"

Sloane rolled over as the September morning sun glared through her window onto her face. "Ugh." A new year and a new school!

A sudden surge of an anxiousness came over her. She ran to the bathroom and threw up.

This was no way to start her morning. Her mother heard her in the bathroom, so she stormed in.

"Sloane, what is going on?"

"Momma, I'm too nervous to go to school today! I can't go—in fact, I won't go!"

"Honey," Momma said, "it is okay to feel nervous. It is a new school and your first day. Once you get to school, you will feel better. Now go get dressed before you miss the bus!"

Sloane put her feelings aside and ran into her room. She threw on a pair of faded blue jeans and a basic white T-shirt, pulled her brown hair back into a ponytail, and ran downstairs as fast as she could.

Her mother asked her if she was going to eat breakfast, but she stormed out of the house.

As she walked up the steps on the bus, she felt that anxiousness come over her again. She looked at everyone sitting down and could not help the uneasy feeling in her stomach, so she threw up in the center aisle of the bus.

Everyone fell silent.

Her face turned bright red. She stood frozen as a statue.

All of a sudden, a sound came from the back of the bus.

"Eww! That girl is throwing up!" someone said. "Hahaha!"

Kids were laughing out loud. Poor Sloane started to cry and ran to the first open seat she could find.

The bus driver stopped the bus and made her way back to see if Sloane was okay.

"Are you okay?" she asked.

Even though she was not okay and was extremely embarrassed, Sloane nodded her head yes.

She just wanted the attention off her. So, the bus driver walked back to her seat, and away to school they went.

When they arrived at school, Sloane rushed off the bus and headed to the first nearby restroom, where she cleaned herself off as much as possible.

Once she cleaned herself up, she looked at herself in the mirror and thought, this is my first day of fifth grade in a new school. Let me try to relax. She closed her eyes, took a few deep breaths, and left the restroom to go to her homeroom class.

As she was walking to her class, she saw three girls from her bus. All three girls were dressed in the latest fashion and had cell phones attached to their hands. Sloane had no doubt that they were the popular clique. As they walked past Sloane, they looked at her and started laughing.

Sloane turned red and kept quiet. Once she got to her homeroom class, she sat down and stared straight ahead at the board. While lost in her own thoughts, she heard a voice from behind and felt a tap on her back.

"Hey." Sloane turned her head to find a girl with freckles, red curly hair, and glasses. "Are you new to this school?" the girl asked.

Sloane nodded and said, "Yes."

"I'm Catherine. What's your name?" the girl asked.

"Sloane," she timidly said and turned around.

Once homeroom ended, Sloane's classes began. She continued keeping to herself and not talking to anyone. Before long she realized it was time for lunch.

As she walked into the cafeteria by herself, she couldn't help but see everyone sitting with their friends eating and talking together. She stood in the lunch line holding her lunch tray in one hand and biting her fingernails.

She grabbed a chocolate milk and a peanut butter and jelly sandwich. After paying for her lunch, she walked to the tables and found a spot to eat by herself.

Although she barely had any appetite, she tried to eat some of her lunch. Then someone walked by and shouted, "Hey, throw-up queen!"

"Do you want to add some extra vomit with a taste of milk to your lunch?" shouted another boy.

Poor Sloane could not handle all the bullying. She began to cry, and her stomach became so sour that she could not eat. She started sweating profusely. Everyone was laughing and staring at her. Everyone except Catherine, who saw her from a distance.

Sloane stood up from her table and ran past Catherine as she flew into the restroom.

Tears flooded the sink that Sloane stood over. Catherine walked into the restroom and saw Sloane in tears.

"What is wrong?" Catherine asked.

"I want to go home! I despise this school!"

Do you want to go to the nurse? Catherine suggested. "Yes," Sloane agreed. "Ok, I will walk you to the nurse" Catherine said.

At the nurse's office Sloane asked the nurse if she could call her momma and tell her she needed to be picked up from school. "I don't feel good," Sloane told the nurse. "I want to go home."

The nurse called Sloane's mom and told her Sloane was not feeling well. "Your mother is on her way, Sloane," she said.

Sloane's mother arrived and picked up Sloane from the nurse's office. She could tell Sloane was upset.

Sloane was silent during the car ride home. "What happened today in school?" Mom asked.

Sloane explained how she felt on the bus and at school and how she became sick and vomited. She told her mom about the racing thoughts in her head. "Everyone in that school makes fun of me when I feel this way! I hate that school, and I never want to go back there!"

Sloane's mom was really struggling with how to respond to Sloane. "This is ridiculous, Sloane! You are going back to school! You better figure out how to control your feelings and get ahold of yourself!"

"Momma, you don't know how I'm feeling! I don't want to be like this!" Sloane shouted.

When they arrived home, Sloane ran into her room. She slammed her bedroom door shut. She felt so hopeless that she got into bed and started to cry.

Her momma was frustrated. She tried to calm down before entering Sloane's room. As she opened Sloane's door. She saw Sloane crying and instantly felt sympathy for her daughter. She laid in bed with her, gave her a hug, and said, "I'm sorry I yelled at you in the car. I know you don't want to act this way. How about I give Dr. Joseph's office a call and see if we can schedule an appointment to see him about the issue you are having?"

Sloane willingly agreed.

The next day Sloane's mother kept her home from school.

She took her to see Dr. Joseph.

"Sloane, how are we doing today?" asked Dr. Joseph.

"I've been better," Sloane said.

"Tell me, what's going on?"

Sloane told Dr. Joseph about her day at school from start to finish. Her momma added in how she had to pick up her daughter from school. Her mother stated that she was concerned for her daughter. She felt hopeless because she did not know how to help her daughter.

Dr. Joseph turned and said to Sloane, "It looks like you have a case of GAD."

"GAD?" said Sloane and her mom. "What is GAD?"

"General anxiety disorder," Dr. Joseph said."

Anxiety is when you feel very worried and think troubling thoughts. Sloane, you were worried yesterday about going to school. You put that thought in your head. No one else did, Sloane."

Sloane became aware of that. "Yes, you are right, Doctor."

"Here's what I want you to do, Sloane," Dr. Joseph said. "I want you to become aware of the thoughts you are thinking and how absurd they are. If you feel that is not helping, take some deep breaths by closing your eyes and inhaling through your nose, expanding your stomach and filling your lungs with air.

Count slowly to five as you inhale. Hold your breath and count to three. Exhale slowly through your mouth and empty your lungs completely. This will release any tension you are feeling. Another exercise you can do is writing down how you are feeling.

Then reading what you wrote back to yourself. By doing this, it enforces positive self-talk and identifying negative thoughts.

Once you are aware of how you feel by doing these exercises you will start to understand yourself better and feel better about yourself. Sloane, Stand up for yourself! Learn to like yourself. You are a smart young girl. Once you do that, people will respect you more. Then you will have a better school year. I want to see you back in my office in two weeks and see how you're doing, Sloane."

"Thank you for making me understand her feelings in a better way," Sloane's mom said.

She jumped out of bed, got dressed, and prepared herself for the day before leaving for the bus. She took some deep breaths sat in her room before leaving. Talking openly to herself and looking into the mirror she reminded herself of how worthy she is. When a negative energy came across her mind, she then fought it back with a positive trait about herself. She then closed her eyes took one last deep breath inhaled all that negative energy then released it all. Opened her eyes and said out loud "Today is going to be a great day."

"Momma came into her room and spoke. "Sloane, I just want you to remember. Every day is a chance to begin again and I want you to start this day new and fresh and have a wonderful day.

"You are right mom. I am worthy and I'm going to make it great!" Sloane said.

When Sloane arrived at the bus, she saw Catherine. "Hi, Sloane."

Sloane looked surprised to see Catherine standing at her bus stop. "I did not know you were at this bus stop. You weren't at this stop on the first day of school?" Sloane said.

"I know," Catherine said. "My mom took me to school on my first day." From here on out I will be at this bus stop!" Sloane was relieved to have a familiar face on the bus with her.

"How are you feeling today?" Catherine asked Sloane.

"I feel better," she said.

"That's great! Hey, do you want to sit together on the bus?" Catherine asked.

"Sure!" Sloane said.

When she got on the bus, Sloane saw the same cool girls in the back that she saw on the first day.

"Hahaha! Hey, Sloane," yelled one of the girls, "did you bring a bucket?"

"A bucket?" Sloane said.

"Yeah, a bucket so you can have something to hold on to when you throw up!"

The other girls laughed.

Sloane's face turned red. She began to sweat and felt nervous. Then she remembered what Dr. Joseph said. She said to herself, Stand up for yourself, Sloane! Sloane looked at the girls and loudly and clearly said, "No one has the right to be rude to me, so mind your own business and worry about yourself!"

The three girls' mouths were wide open in disbelief! They fell silent. Sloane sat down next to Catherine.

Catherine laughed. "Good going Sloane. You finally stood up for yourself."

At first Sloane wasn't sure how to feel about what just happened, but then she realized that she had finally stood up for herself. She felt surprisingly proud of herself. She smirked and said to Catherine, "Here is to a better year ahead," and she gave her a high five as the school bus drove off to school.

About the Author

Dana M. Shickora is a first time author who lives in Mullica Hill, New Jersey, with her husband, two children, and her dog. Due to the Coronavirus pandemic, she found time to fulfill her lifelong dream of being a writer. She has been a Registered Medical Assistant/Phlebotomist for over fifteen years in the healthcare system.

Printed in the United States
by Baker & Taylor Publisher Services